IGNITING REVIVAL

IGNITING REVIVAL

A 21 Day Prayer Guide for Revival Preparation

Scott Hamby
Edited by Dr. H.D. McCarty

THE HOLY BIBLE, NEW INTERNATIONAL VERSION®, NIV® Copyright © 1973, 1978, 1984, 2011 by Biblica, Inc.® Used by permission. All rights reserved worldwide.

Copyright © 2018 SCOTT HAMBY
Published by SCOTT HAMBY

All rights reserved. No part of this publication may be reproduced, stored in a retrieval system or transmitted, in any form, or by any means, electronic, mechanical, recorded, photocopied, or otherwise, without the prior written permission of both the copyright owner and the above publisher of this book, except by a reviewer who may quote brief passages in a review.

The scanning, uploading, and distribution of this book via the Internet or via any other means without the permission of the publisher is illegal and punishable by law. Please purchase only authorized electronic editions and do not participate in or encourage electronic piracy of copyrightable materials. Your support of the author's rights is appreciated.

Designed by Vince Pannullo
Printed in the United States of America
by RJ Communications.

ISBN: 978-0-578-20922-7

Contents

DAY 1: Why Do I Want Revival? 23
    A need for personal revival

DAY 2: So What, "God loves me"? 27
    Desensitized to God

DAY 3: Encountering…. 31
    Need for a personal encounter with God's holiness

DAY 4: He's Just God 37
    We must revere God

DAY 5: It's My Decision 43
    Surrendering to God

DAY 6: He Is Accountable to Who? 47
    God's sovereignty

DAY 7: Ah, There is a Theme 51
    Justice is required

DAY 8: What is repentance? 55
    Time for U-turn and abandonment

DAY 9: Struggling with sin... 61
    Being on auto-pilot

DAY 10: Sin Makes a Better Testimony! 67
    Sinning must stop

DAY 11: Is There a Difference? 71
    A need for weeping, sacrifice, and repentance
DAY 12: God Calls Me to Do What?? 77
    Wrestling with repentance
DAY 13: I See You 81
    Seeing temptation for what it is
DAY 14: Out of this World 85
    Struggle against evil
Day 15: Tools Included, Part 1 89
    Understanding the Armor of God
Day 16: Tools Included, Part 2 93
    Understanding the Armor of God
Day 17: No One is an Island 99
    The church is an army who can win together
Day 18: The Power of Prayer 103
    Pray to discover and move to His will
Day 19: Getting Usable 109
    Forgiveness is not optional
Day 20: The Rules 113
    Which rules are you living by?
Day 21: Hope 119
    Revival has begun

A Final Word 123

This book is dedicated to God the Father, Jesus the Son and the Holy Spirit and their work in bringing a spiritual awakening in the 21st Century.

Acknowledgements

MANY people have helped make this writing possible. I must say thank you to several of them:

- Julie, my wife, for being patient with me and helping to prepare this for the people of God.
- Ernie and Pat, my father and mother, for always encouraging me to love and serve God in the fulfillment of my calling.
- Rob and Stacie Bratcher, our friends, for listening to all the ideas and offering sound guidance to reach an effective tool.
- Wade Samples, our "mountain-home pastor," who always strengthens us through his faith.
- Dr. H.D. McCarty for his tutelage, support and contribution to my ministry and this writing.
- Claude King for his gracious work in editorial comments and forward remarks.

Forward

WE are at a critical time in our nation where we are being shaken to the very foundations of our civil society. People are experiencing significant stress, anxiety, and even horror over mass shootings, serial bombings, natural disasters, the consequences of addictions that are claiming tens of thousands of lives annually, the polarization of people who are different from one another, harassment and abuse in the workplace, economic uncertainty, the challenge of distinguishing between truth and deception in our media, and even the security of our democratic processes that are foundational to our nation's government. Historically, times like these have been ripe for seasons of revival and spiritual awakening. When people are yearning for and seeking stability, security, truth, and hope, and peace, they find that God is their only source for solutions that last.

You may feel like Israel when they said, "The LORD has forsaken me, the Lord has forgotten me? (Isa. 49:14, NIV). But there comes a time when God announces: 'In the time of my favor I heard you, and in the day of salvation I helped you.' I tell you, now is the time of God's favor, now is the day of salvation" (2 Cor. 6:2, NIV). I believe we are approaching such a time. What we need is a revival among God's people as they return to Him. Then God has a people through which Spirit empowered witness bears fruit in a spiritual harvest.

I remember a statement in a song sung during the Jesus Movement that said, "It only takes a spark to get a fire going" (*Pass It On* by Kurt Kaiser, 1969). Revival can start with you and with your church. Our nation may be increasingly becoming a tinderbox ready for a spiritual spark. Would you present yourself to the Lord to become such a spark? Where do we begin?

David Bryant, founder of Concerts of Prayer International, once said, "My job is to take people to God, and He can take them from there." I believe that is what Scott Hamby is seeking to do in *Igniting Revival*. He is pointing you to God and His Word. He is encouraging you to pray about matters that concern the Lord and what He desires to do to revive His people. If you will seek the Lord with all your heart, He will be found by you. I encourage you to join Scott on this 21-day journey toward igniting revival in your heart and your church. When God speaks to you through His Word and by His Holy Spirit, obey Him. Make the necessary adjustments to become an instrument through which God can work. Prepare yourself so when Jesus commands, "Let down your nets for a catch," you can respond and join Him in a great spiritual harvest.

Claude V. King, Coauthor of
Experiencing God and *Fresh Encounter:
God's Pattern for Revival and Spiritual Awakening.*

Introduction

DEFINITIONS are required to ensure understanding is gained from these readings. Many people of many religions use the same words, but envision very different conclusions. The following words hold these definitions in this context of this book. These definitions are simplistic and not intended to be a scholarly dissertation, but do have theological implications. Further study is continuously required by all who truly hunger to be students and learners of the written Word (scripture). This is our first great step to make real our love for the Living Word (Jesus). Only then does a believer become a student of the Bible. My opening comments follow these definitions.

God: Yahweh. I AM. Known in three persons as God the Father, God the Son and God the Holy Spirit. The Godhead has made us in His triune image and is revealing to us what that means.

Jesus: The Son of God. The human incarnation of the Godhead on earth. Sinless. Fully divine and fully human, simultaneously. The Messiah (Hebrew), Christ (Greek) of the Father. The Son was sent to reveal to mankind the grace (love) and truth (reality) of the Father.

Holy Spirit: The person of the Godhead who indwells all born again persons for the purpose of aiding his/her spiritual growth, communication with the Godhead and conformation to the imagery of Christ.

Cross: the means of execution by which Jesus Christ died to provide atonement (forgiveness) and propitiation (satisfaction) for human sin, which was and is completed, confirmed and communicated by His resurrection. The cross is a symbol for those who are born again of the moment of their salvation and marks the beginning of their journey in sanctification (growing in holy living) and Lordship (submission of whatever is necessary to completely and continually follow Jesus).

Grace: receiving a pardon which one does not deserve or has not earned.

Mercy: not receiving punishment which one does deserve.

Justice: legally, that which is required to satisfy a violation of law, the consequence of which is delivered through judgment. Biblically, humans are sinful by default in their nature as a result of the Fall and as such are in violation of God's law (His holiness). Therefore, justice for this violation is condemnation to eternal separation from the Godhead and is required. The judgment resulting from holy justice is the total absence, with exception of wrath, of the Lord from the unholy creation.

Prayer: a two-way conversation and dialogue in which the believer is totally honest and open with the Lord, and the Lord reveals Himself, purposes or direction. An activity through which a believer's will is bent to God's will, not vice versa.

Holy: purity and separation to Truth. Whole perfection. To be set apart from all evil in order to please the Lord and serve Him significantly.

Truth: that which is absolute, fact and real regardless of human opinion or perspective. Biblically refers to God's purposes of creation, Jesus' work of salvation, and the Holy Spirit's work of sanctification. God's standards of reality that cannot be ignored.

Christ-like living: the development of a relationship with the Savior that increasingly produces intimacy with Him, fulfillment of His will and a pursuit of a sinless life that is motivated by and demonstrates the Godhead's love.

Humility: the opposite of promoting oneself and desires. The making of oneself as nothing, as our Lord did, to be totally available to the will of God.

Pruning: a process through which one is spiritually disciplined by God or the Holy Spirit reveals the need to remove more of one's self to deeper sanctification and Christ-like living. This is often painful, difficult and requires sacrifice. Nevertheless, the result produces a deeper more robust relationship with the Godhead creating a more abundant and joyful Christian life. This type of life does not mean the absence of further pruning, challenges, persecution, trials or temptations.

Revival: the spiritual renewal of a Christian's heart. The exciting return of a Christian back to their first love. A revitalization of life of a Christian resulting from him/her falling on his/her knees in repentance of sin at the foot of the cross, relinquishing him/herself wholly to Christ-like living, and rejoicing in the abundant life promised. In essence, the exchange of a person's mind for Christ's mind.

Spiritual Awakening: a large movement in which many spiritually dead awaken to the need for spiritual change and are brought to new life in Jesus that results in a culture shift back to God's standards of morality and wisdom.

As the world continues to erupt in wars, religious sects go to new lows of reprobate violence, our nation gets louder about denying and rejecting God, and interest in church plummets – the need for spiritual revival grows exponentially. But, is a revival enough or have we reached the threshold of need for a spiritual awakening? Indeed the answer is yes! We need an awakening that causes a culture shift as the people of God return to the cross in total sin abandonment and holy Christ-like living because we rediscover God's great love for us.

Yet our churches have waned on holding revival meetings over the last few decades. Some have said revival meetings are old programing that does not work anymore. Others have said these kinds of meetings cannot be effective in reaching a technology based society with busy schedules. Churches have opted for newer programs or simply not filled the gap created by removing the services. The scriptural calling of Evangelist has been marred by many televangelists who preach(ed) a gospel other than Christ alone or others who abuse(d) its purity for some distorted view of power or financial gain.

The evidence is clear. Without God indwelling and guiding man's heart, man will never choose the moral, noble and loving path.

Christians need to be flocking to churches, small groups and individual prayer closets in fervent prayer, fasting and worship yielding themselves to Christ's Lordship and then entreating Him for a spiritual awakening. This large scale revival will come when the people of God follow the path identified by God Himself in 2 Chronicles 7:14. Though this has been quoted numerous times, it never loses its eternal power. "If my people, who are called by my name, will humble themselves and pray and seek my face and turn from their wicked ways, then will I hear from heaven and will forgive their sin and heal their land." (New International Version)

Christians, this means true repentance and brokenness without regard of pride, fervently seeking of The Kingdom first, relinquishing all we are and have to His Lordship, living revitalized in holiness in a spiritually destitute world; then God will pour out spiritual awakening! Pruning is required, the cost is high and the path is narrow, but the reward is eternal and available here on earth and in heaven. Enter these following days of preparation with a pliable heart, open mind and commitment to follow the Lord's leading. These devotions are laden with scripture references to jump start your study; be sure to read them and search for other relevant passages as the Bible is the authoritative word of God, not this study guide. Being in The Living Word, that is Jesus, and studying the written word, that is the Bible, can bring revival.

Over the next 21 days, I want you to join me on a journey toward personal revival with a prayer for corporate revival in our churches and spiritual awakening in our community and nation. Each day I'll point you to God's Word and challenge you to engage a revival topic. Then I'm going to recommend an action you can take to begin this personal return to the Lord that leads to transformation. Each day also has an area for you to write items such as obedience to what you have read from the Bible, or to note a personal prayer about the topic that day, or simply to keep a personal journal during this journey. What you write is up to you, however, it is critical that you reflect in writing what God is speaking to you about. A historical record of God's work in you is a great testimony to Him, demonstrates answered prayer and encourages you in future difficult times. Let's get started!

DAY 1

WHY DO I WANT REVIVAL?

A NEED FOR PERSONAL REVIVAL

TODAY many things demand our attention: family, job, politics, hobbies, friends, world events, church and on and on. In our home it means both parents work, three kids with activities (high school, middle school and elementary), roles at church, grandparents and attempting to maintain a social life. To make matters worse, these demands come instantaneously on our mobile devices. Always connected, always listening, and always responding. Focusing on one thing at a time is just not the way we live. We focus on multiple things at once. It has become our American culture.

Another part of that culture is to be self-sufficient. We have a "can do" attitude and *can do* it on our own. Not just one thing, but multiple things and do them instantly. We rely on our tools to get us through the day, not other people. And, if we're honest, not on God either or maybe not as much as we need to anyway. If only there was a "God App!"

Revival is more than just an event happening at church; something you go to and check the box for attendance. Revival is to be a daily and repeatable event in our lives. We are to pray continually (1 Thessalonians 5:17) and pray in the Spirit on all occasions (Ephesians 6:18). Through prayer we are to daily put on the Armor of God (Ephesians 6:11). We are to praise God day after day (Psalms 96:2). We must realign our focus on God (Philippians 4:4-8; Colossians 3:1-17).

This need for realignment is why we should want revival, because life's activities have reduced our relationship with the Father to a check box on a task list. We are no longer living in the dynamic, intimate relationship He designed us to be in with Him. Genesis 2 describes the Lord God "forming" man, which suggests a more intimate process, whereas in chapter 1 He "created" and "made" everything else. The Father then planted a garden just for His crowning creation; a place of beauty and provision where He could walk with Adam and Eve. He did all this for humans alone. The Father wants this kind of relationship with us too. Revival can revitalize our relationship with Him.

As you enter this first week, take note the study is focused on God the Father, who He is, and the proper perspective we must have about His character and purpose.

Take Action

Take the time right now to make a calendar entry in your phone or on your wall calendar for regular quiet time with God for the next 20 days to do just that—meet with Him. It will not be easy; pruning never is. Unforeseen events will pop up to redirect your commitment to meet with God; resist the distraction. Make the *decision* now to bend, break or remove your will, understanding, or emotions in order to be open to the Spirit's voice in your quiet time. This journey to personal revival can spill over into corporate revival as individual members agree to join together in personal journey for these 21 days. Then the scheduled event of revival meetings will rain down with God's glory and blessings.

Pause and pray for your growth, openness and personal revival in the next 20 days.

Scripture

"Yet you, LORD, are our Father. We are the clay, you are the potter; we are all the work of your hand." Isaiah 64:8 NIV

Notes for the day:

(Here is where you can write items such as obedience to what you have read from the Bible, or to note a personal prayer about the topic of the day, or simply to keep a personal journal during the journey.)

DAY 2

SO WHAT, "GOD LOVES ME"

DESENSITIZED TO GOD

Do you have a favorite seat in church? Let's ask it this way: if someone wants to invite you to lunch, discuss a Bible study lesson question, or request you to help out in the nursery do they know they can find you in the 5th pew, in the center section on the left end? Then you *do* have a seat with your name on it! I am guilty of this too! This is where you have watched Christmas plays, Easter programs, and the pastor preach week after week. You know who is sitting in front of you and behind you. It may even be the way your pastor takes a quick survey of attendance! Ever wondered how he knew you missed last Sunday?

We are creatures of habit in more ways than this, though. We drive the same path to work, eat at the same restaurants, buy the same food at the store and *hear the same words at church*. Words and phrases like, "God loves you" or "Jesus died for you" or "God is holy" or "take up your cross." These all get tossed into the same bucket in our mind labeled "Church Lingo." The meaning of them fades away as does their impact. We hear it, we believe it and we even value it, but our statements, even right and sincere, do not seem to shake our world, change our lifestyle, or influence our choices like they once did.

Here is where you make the decision to let them in again. God does love you because He sent His Son to die in place of you for the consequences you deserve, and it is because God IS Holy. These concepts should cause you to feel weak at the knees, fill your eyes with a flood of tears and heart pound out of your chest because you do not have to be scourged, spit on, mocked or hung for your choices against God's will for your life (a.k.a. sin).

Take Action

This is time in today's study for you to pause and focus on these ideas, these facts. The time is now for you to place value back into the salvation gift God has given you through Jesus the Christ. It is time for you to remember the hope that comes from this eternal work. Let His mind and desires shake your world, change your lifestyle and influence your choices.

Scripture

"¹⁶ For God so loved the world that he gave his one and only Son, that whoever believes in him shall not perish but have eternal life. ¹⁷ For God did not send his Son into the world to condemn the world, but to save the world through him. ¹⁸ Whoever believes in him is not condemned, but whoever does not believe stands condemned already because they have not believed in the name of God's one and only Son." John 3:16-18 NIV

Mediate on what this means for you. Thank God for his gift of salvation.

Notes for the day:

DAY 3

Encountering….

Need for a personal encounter with God's holiness

I remember as a junior high student hearing my parents announce that my Dad had cancer. They quickly said the doctor was hopeful it could be overcome, but there was still a possibility he could die from it. My feelings ran wild. It became hard for me to focus in school, challenging for me to work in church and made my daily routine difficult. Then we received news that the treatments had been successful to send the cancer into remission. A few years later I went off to college. While there, the news came the cancer had returned and was worse than before. Within months there was a call to come home because he had passed away.

I, like most people, knew what cancer was, believed it existed and understood intellectually what it meant. That was everything I needed to declare I knew cancer. But I was proven wrong. Encountering cancer showed me I knew nothing about it. All my head knowledge was nice, but insufficient for it to impact my life. What we believe about God is no different.

God is holy! What does that mean to you? We speak of it in church, we know what it means and we believe it. That's enough, isn't it? No! Until we ***encounter*** God's holiness it will never impact our life. We need to understand that His holiness is a driving factor. It is because He is holy the Seraphim worship Him 24/7 declaring "Holy, holy, holy is the LORD Almighty;" God set limits around Mount Saini for the Israelites; the whole earth quaked at the death of Jesus; and the reason God will cast Satan into Hell for eternity. His holiness is why He is intolerant of sin and why death is the price of sin. Holiness is what demands justice of sin and why justice is carried out in judgment that condemns mankind to hell, eternally separated from God.

You see, when God created Adam and Eve they were perfect, sinless. Genesis 3:8-9 tells us that the Lord God was walking in the garden with an expectation that Adam and Eve would join Him. Why else would He call out to them? It was normal for God to be with Adam and Eve. Then in the rest of Chapter 3 we see sin called out by God. Among the consequences was separation and banishment from God's presence, which was the most severe of them all. Their sinful status has passed down from one generation to another for all of past time. (Romans 5:17-19) We all therefore receive the same consequence as they did:

separation from God on earth and in eternity because He is holy and must satisfy His wrath against sin. Sin is what broke the relationship between man and God. Romans 6:23 tells us that the consequence of sin is death, that is separation from God forever. We also learn there that God made a way to overcome that break, it was through the death, burial and resurrection of His son Jesus. See also Romans 5:6-11. The only way to restore a perfect and holy relationship is for a perfect human to overcome the barrier of death according to Hebrews 4:15, 7:26 and other passages. In 2 Corinthians 5:21 we learn that Jesus was perfect, in Matthew 1:18-25 He was human and in Revelation 5 he overcame death physically and spiritually.

Justice is for all mankind to be sentenced to hell, but God saw fit to reconcile His creation with Himself. This is where love, grace and mercy come in. As believers bearing the righteousness of Jesus, we can enter into the presence of God and His holiness. God is holy, and we must be holy to be with Him. Praise the Lord Jesus Christ for making this possible!

Take Action

We will examine this more, but for today pray that God will open your eyes and heart to His holiness. Read Isaiah 6:1-4 and pray for an encounter of holiness.

Scripture

"In the year that King Uzziah died, I saw the Lord, high and exalted, seated on a throne; and the train of his robe filled the temple. ² Above him were seraphim, each with six wings: With two wings they covered their faces, with two they covered their feet, and with two they were flying. ³ And they were calling to one another:

"Holy, holy, holy is the L<small>ORD</small> Almighty; the whole earth is full of his glory."

⁴ At the sound of their voices the doorposts and thresholds shook and the temple was filled with smoke." Isaiah 6:1-4 NIV

Notes for the day:

_____
_____
_____
_____
_____
_____
_____
_____
_____
_____
_____
_____
_____
_____
_____

DAY 4

HE'S JUST GOD

WE MUST REVERE GOD

CAN you think of a time you met a V.I.P.? Maybe the C.E.O. of a corporation, the founder of a well-known Foundation, or the Governor of your state? Have you ever thought of how you would act if you could meet the President of the United States or the recent Pulitzer Prize winner? These positions grant the holder immediate respect and on some level, homage. We want to be around them because they are important and we secretly hope that some of that will be imputed to us.

God is greater than any V.I.P. No matter what name you can call out from history, they pale in comparison to God. Man's best never reaches God's standard. Man's inventions over time have been impressive and some have even changed the course of history. Yet God, with only words, spoke the world into existence. Not only the world, but our universe, galaxy and space beyond. With only His words falling from His lips trillions of stars came to be. With only His words the coloring of butterflies emerged.

With only His words man and woman were made in His image. How amazing is that?!

We forget too easily how great God really is! We reduce him to a vending machine for answers, as the "man upstairs" who might be listening, or the universe police officer waiting to catch you in some offense. God is not any of these. So, who is He?

Take Action

Read the segments from Genesis 1 below. Today contemplate on these names of God. Using your Bible's concordance or digital Bible's search feature, search them out in the Scriptures as this is not a complete list. Give homage to God:

Yahweh, Holy One, Living God, Lord of Lords, Deliverer, Messiah, Light of the World, Creator, Sure Foundation, King of Glory, Good Shepherd, Prince of Peace, WORD, Ruler, God Almighty, Master, Lion of Judah, Advocate, Second Adam, Wonderful Counselor, Abba Father, Immanuel, The First and the Last, …. I AM.

Scripture

¹ In the beginning God created the heavens and the earth. ² Now the earth was formless and empty, darkness was over the surface of the deep, and the Spirit of God was hovering over the waters. ³ And God said, "Let there be light," and there was light. ⁴ God saw that the light was

good, and he separated the light from the darkness…. [6] And God said, "Let there be a vault between the waters to separate water from water." [7] So God made the vault and separated the water under the vault from the water above it. And it was so…. [9] And God said, "Let the water under the sky be gathered to one place, and let dry ground appear." And it was so….And God saw that it was good.

[11] Then God said, "Let the land produce vegetation: seed-bearing plants and trees on the land that bear fruit with seed in it, according to their various kinds." And it was so…. [14] And God said, "Let there be lights in the vault of the sky to separate the day from the night….And it was so. [16] God made two great lights—the greater light to govern the day and the lesser light to govern the night. He also made the stars….And God saw that it was good.

[20] And God said, "Let the water teem with living creatures, and let birds fly above the earth across the vault of the sky." [21] So God created the great creatures of the sea and every living thing with which the water teems and that moves about in it, according to their kinds, and every winged bird according to its kind. And God saw that it was good….

[24] And God said, "Let the land produce living creatures according to their kinds: the livestock, the creatures that move along the ground, and the wild animals, each according to its kind." And it was so…. [26] Then God said, "Let us make mankind in our image, in our likeness, so that they may rule over the fish in the sea and the birds

in the sky, over the livestock and all the wild animals, and over all the creatures that move along the ground."

[27] So God created mankind in his own image, in the image of God he created them; male and female he created them.

[28] God blessed them and said to them, "Be fruitful and increase in number; fill the earth and subdue it. Rule over the fish in the sea and the birds in the sky and over every living creature that moves on the ground." ….[31] God saw all that he had made, and it was very good. And there was evening, and there was morning—the sixth day.

2[1] Thus the heavens and the earth were completed in all their vast array.[2] By the seventh day God had finished the work he had been doing; so on the seventh day he rested from all his work." Genesis 1:1 -- 2:2 NIV

Notes for the day:

DAY 5

IT'S MY DECISION

SURRENDERING TO GOD

CHOICE. It is the basis of our marketplace and our lifestyle. Walk into a department store for a new shirt and spend hours searching the racks for just the right one. Walk into an electronics store and spend half a day piecing together the ultimate technology package integrating your mobile device with the TV, refrigerator, baby monitor and your watch. Sit down at your favorite restaurant and stall the server three times as you struggle to select the tastiest platter.

Choice drives our culture's marketing, shopping, corporations and even our churches. Ever been "shopping" for a church? Most of us have at one point or another. We have gotten accustomed to making choices for ourselves. We get upset when we cannot have what we want. Making our own choice has become woven into the fabric of our culture, yet it is the opposite of what we are called to do under His Lordship.

As a true believer, our choice (that is, our want) is

irrelevant (Hebrews 12:1-11; James 4:1-10; and others). Our will should be to do His will. We must learn to yield ourselves to God and His plans for Kingdom advancement and our involvement in this magnificent drama. This is the only choice we can make if we call ourselves Christians (John 14:23-24; 15:1-11; Acts 5:29-32; Romans 2:13; 1 John 2:3; 1 John 5:3; and others). This choice is obedience. This choice is sacrifice. This choice is not for personal gain. This choice is costly (Matthew 9: 57-62; Luke 14:25-33; and others). This choice will yield spiritual fruit and blessings beyond our imagination.

Take Action

Today read Matthew 26:36-46 below and reflect on the choices made by Jesus and the disciples. The Lord Jesus chose to fulfill the Father's plan at the greatest cost. The disciples chose to please their flesh with sleep. What choice will you make? Pray and dialogue about your choice, asking the Father to help you. Determine you will be "strong in the grace that is in Christ Jesus" (2 Tim 2:1) and fight caving into your physical weaknesses.

Scripture

"[36] Then Jesus went with his disciples to a place called Gethsemane, and he said to them, "Sit here while I go over there and pray." [37] He took Peter and the two sons of Zebedee along with him, and he began to be sorrowful and troubled. ³⁸ Then he said to them, "My soul is overwhelmed with sorrow to the point of death. Stay here and keep watch with me."

³⁹ Going a little farther, he fell with his face to the ground and prayed, "My Father, if it is possible, may this cup be taken from me. Yet not as I will, but as you will."

⁴⁰ Then he returned to his disciples and found them sleeping. "Couldn't you men keep watch with me for one hour?" he asked Peter. ⁴¹ "Watch and pray so that you will not fall into temptation. The spirit is willing, but the flesh is weak."

⁴² He went away a second time and prayed, "My Father, if it is not possible for this cup to be taken away unless I drink it, may your will be done."

⁴³ When he came back, he again found them sleeping, because their eyes were heavy. ⁴⁴ So he left them and went away once more and prayed the third time, saying the same thing.

⁴⁵ Then he returned to the disciples and said to them, "Are you still sleeping and resting? Look, the hour has come, and the Son of Man is delivered into the hands of sinners. ⁴⁶ Rise! Let us go! Here comes my betrayer!"
Matthew 26:36-46 NIV

Notes for the day:

DAY 6

HE IS ACCOUNTABLE TO WHO?

GOD'S SOVEREIGNTY

TO whom are you accountable? Accountability is defined as being required or expected to justify actions or decisions. For many people this idea brings resentment, anger, fear or other negative feelings. "I don't answer to anyone" seems to be the mantra in today's society. Accountability…well that is just archaic.

Nonetheless, we are accountable. We must obey the law or answer to the crime. We must make the right choices for our family or our children go without food, shelter, clothing or mental and spiritual protection. We have a boss, a spouse, a friend, parents and others in our lives who expect things from us and when we do not perform they look for justification and explanation of why and what happened.

God, however, is accountable to no one. Take a moment to think on that. For some, that statement may sting and make you think you are not going to read any further. But for others, this statement rings in your heart as true and in your mind as sovereign. A couple of days ago we looked at who the Father really is, recall the list of names? One of His attributes is that He is Sovereign. God is God, not god. Isaiah 46:9-10 NIV says, "I am God, and there is no other; I am God, and there is none like me. I make known the end from the beginning, from ancient times, what is still to come. I say: My purpose will stand, and I will do all that I please."

Our God declares His sovereignty throughout the scriptures. When we read the Bible from cover to cover we see Him orchestrating humans, nations, animals, angels, the stars, the timeline, and even life and death for whomever, wherever, and whenever He decides. The Lord God declares, "I am the Alpha and the Omega. Who is, and who was, and who is to come, THE ALMIGHTY." (Revelation 1:8 NIV) And again, "I am the Alpha and the Omega, the First and the Last, the Beginning and the End." (Revelation 22:13 NIV)

Take Action

Wise and triumphant are those in creation who acknowledge the Creator for who He is. We must shift our commonly arrogant mindset from our greatness to His greatness. Revival comes when we are humble, know our place, take up our cross, worship as the Seraphim worship declaring "Holy, Holy, Holy" and trust control of our lives to Him. Will you pray today that God would give you peace so that you may accept His sovereignty?

Scripture

"[13]Your kingdom is an everlasting kingdom, and your dominion endures through all generations. The Lord is trustworthy in all he promises and faithful in all he does." Psalms 145:13 NIV

"[5] Trust in the LORD with all your heart and lean not on your own understanding; [6] in all your ways submit to him, and he will make your paths straight." Proverbs 3:5-6 NIV

Notes for the day:

_____

_____

_____

_____

_____

_____

_____

_____

_____

_____

_____

_____

_____

DAY 7

AH, THERE IS A THEME

JUSTICE IS REQUIRED

IF you have not discovered it yet, this first week of prayer is focused on God the Father, who He is, and the proper perspective we must have about His character and purpose. This is the starting point. Without seeking to understand and *accept* who our Creator Lord is, we will never encounter Him. If we cannot encounter Him, we will never see revival individually or as a body of believers. Revival is just as the word says, to recall attention to or represent something from long ago; to make alive again. If you are born again, then at one time Jesus our Savior through the Holy Spirit showed you your sin and you fell at the cross in repentance. At that moment, you began to have a proper perspective of God.

The fact is that The Church has lost the proper perspective of who the Godhead is and what He is about. This vacuum presents a significant spiritual diminishment that results in dead-end living! To relinquish oneself to another is a frightening feeling. To identify oneself as a subject to someone else makes us very uncomfortable. To yield our choices and will to a person other than ourselves breeds defiance. These are human emotions fostered by a culture that does not know the Lord God and are ignorant of and indifferent to His significance.

As Christians we must see the Godhead for who He is. It is because of who He is that Jesus was required to die. As the sovereign, holy and perfect God, **justice** is required of sin. Sin must receive judgment. The only escape is through grace and mercy from the same God; **grace** to be given what we do not deserve – to bear Christ's righteousness and live eternally in heaven with Him – and **mercy** from what we do deserve – damnation in hell eternally separated from Him; spiritual death.

Justice is the page on which grace and mercy are written. It is only through justice that our Savior's love, of which we speak so fondly, truly gains its meaning and value (Rm. 3:21-26, 5:8). It was love irrevocably tethered to justice that held Jesus to the cross, not the nails! Jesus understood "it is the blood that makes atonement for one's life" (Lev. 17:11 NIV) so that our relationship with the Father could be restored (Rm 5). If the Father's holiness did not demand justice because His love alone was able to overcome sin, then Jesus would not have had to die on the cross, and we could have been received into heaven at no cost. This, however, is not the truth as a sacrifice was required, according to Hebrews 10: 1-14 et al., because the wages of sin is death, as Romans 6:23

tells us; a bloody and brutal death preceded by scourging, spitting, mocking and betrayal. Yet Jesus' prayer, through drops of blood in the garden of Gethsemane, was, "Not my will, but yours!"

Take Action

As you close this first week of study, deeply evaluate your position with your Lord and Savior. Read Isaiah's response to the glimpse of Jesus' glory in chapter 6 verse 5. With sincerity, a genuine heart, fear, trembling and hope cry out to the LORD over your sin. Let us all taste again the wonder of the life our Master wants us to live! Let a new song of revival begin!

Scripture

[5] "Woe to me!" I cried. "I am ruined! For I am a man of unclean lips, and I live among a people of unclean lips, and my eyes have seen the King, the LORD Almighty." Isaiah 6:5 NIV

Notes for the day:

DAY 8

WHAT IS REPENTANCE?

TIME FOR U-TURN AND ABANDONMENT

"I am sorry." Three simple words. Three impossible words for many. Ever watched someone struggle to utter these words? The body language is obvious. Kids yell it in response to parental directive to speak it to a sibling or friend. Teenagers, well, getting them to say anything is a challenge, let alone an apology. Many adults reject anything that places ownership or blame on themselves. Why do we struggle with this so much?

This struggle extends to our spiritual life too. If we say anything at all about it to God, we ask "to be forgiven of all our sins," so we do not have to list them. One prayer does it all, right? If we had to list them or worse yet, let the Spirit call them out to us, we would cringe and hide; then avoid time with God. We want to be seen as good. We want to think the best of ourselves, at least before

God, if nowhere else. We think we need God to see us in a positive way so He'll answer our prayers.

The problem with that line of thinking is that God sees everything, and the only one we're truly fooling is ourselves. God is very clear throughout the scriptures about His *conditional* response. The Mosaic Covenant (Deuteronomy 28) stated from God that if the people obeyed Him, then they would receive blessings, but if they disobeyed Him He would curse them, scatter them among the nations and make them shameful before the whole earth. (Ezekiel 22, Daniel. 9:1-19) When Jesus came, a new covenant was instituted, but with the same conditional response. Repentance was, and is required to receive forgiveness (Mark 1:15, Luke 13:1-5; Acts 3:19, Revelation 2:5, 3:19, and others.) Therefore we must remember, ponder and make an honest response to Hebrews 4:13, "Nothing in all creation is hidden from God's sight. Everything is uncovered and laid bare before the eyes of him to who we must give an account." (NIV)

Repentance? Wait, we started this discussion about just saying, "I'm sorry," not about repentance. True, but, for a Christian repentance is the measure, saying, "I'm sorry" is not. Daily admission of wrong doing and asking His forgiveness; repentance, meaning 180 degrees of a 'U-turn;' **abandonment** of the sin; and warring against its return: this is what God requires. We must have a broken heart with intention and hope of decreasing our weaknesses and desire for rebellion. Our confession to the Lord of our sickness over our sin will lead us to act on His promise found in 1 John 1:9. Much more could be said here on this topic, but for now prayerfully consider this concept of repentance in your life as you read today's scripture.

Take Action

Read Romans 6:1-14. Pray that the Holy Spirit will show you your sins, one by one; then repent of them and actively seek the Holy Spirit to help you no longer be enslaved to them.

Scripture

"[1] What shall we say, then? Shall we go on sinning so that grace may increase? [2] By no means! We are those who have died to sin; how can we live in it any longer? [3] Or don't you know that all of us who were baptized into Christ Jesus were baptized into his death? [4] We were therefore buried with him through baptism into death in order that, just as Christ was raised from the dead through the glory of the Father, we too may live a new life.

[5] For if we have been united with him in a death like his, we will certainly also be united with him in a resurrection like his. [6] For we know that our old self was crucified with him so that the body ruled by sin might be done away with, that we should no longer be slaves to sin— [7] because anyone who has died has been set free from sin.

⁸ Now if we died with Christ, we believe that we will also live with him. ⁹ For we know that since Christ was raised from the dead, he cannot die again; death no longer has mastery over him. ¹⁰ The death he died, he died to sin once for all; but the life he lives, he lives to God.

¹¹ In the same way, count yourselves dead to sin but alive to God in Christ Jesus. ¹² Therefore do not let sin reign in your mortal body so that you obey its evil desires. ¹³ Do not offer any part of yourself to sin as an instrument of wickedness, but rather offer yourselves to God as those who have been brought from death to life; and offer every part of yourself to him as an instrument of righteousness. ¹⁴ For sin shall no longer be your master, because you are not under the law, but under grace." Romans 6:1-14 NIV

Notes for the day:

DAY 9

STRUGGLING WITH SIN

BEING ON AUTO-PILOT

HAVE you ever found yourself on auto-pilot as you drive home? Originally, you planned to go somewhere else before returning home. For instance, you needed to get milk from the store or needed to drop something off at a friend's house, but instead you drove straight home. Pulled into the driveway, and maybe even got inside the house. Then it hits you like a ton of bricks: "I had to go to…" Back into the car you go!

Waging war against sin is much the same. For each of us *that sin,* which is our personal Achilles heel, is different. Paul reminds us, "the old has gone, the new has come." (2 Corinthians 5:17 NIV). The result of repentance is a daily choice to avoid circumstances in which we can be tempted and easily swayed to commit sin. This is the *new* part that has come, which Paul refers to in 2 Corinthians 5:17. Because the Holy Spirit lives in us, our desires change, shift, and morph into what God desires. For some sins, we give them up, and seem hardly impacted. But for other sins, we scratch and claw through our lives to escape their hold on us. This is where the daily renewal of our minds and hearts becomes so important.

Auto-pilot sends us down the path of our old ways, and if we do not take overt and decisive action to ingrain a new path, we will frequently find ourselves in disobedience. We then need to process through conviction, confession, and correction. The issue here is sanctification, which means we advance and grow under and in the Lordship of Christ. As we expand our thinking and maturity in our understanding of who the Lord Jesus really is and how He works, we yield and surrender more and more to the leadership, authority and protection.

Take Action

The Apostle Paul discusses this very struggle in Romans 7:12-25. Read through this today, more than once, as it is a lot to digest and understand. Do not rush through it. The content and intent of the words is robust and deep. Pray fervently for God to help you in your continuous struggle with sin. Know that any and all sin can be overcome through Jesus Christ our Lord!

Dr. H.D. McCarty offers these encouraging words about this struggle: "We must not let Satan accuse and discourage us when we sin! The Lord knows what we're not, but loves us anyway and always offers us renewal. We have no idea how really sinful and self-centered we are. We must confess, trust His promise and get on with the Christian life. I have learned that even my repentance needs to be repented of."

Scripture

"¹² So then, the law is holy, and the commandment is holy, righteous and good.

¹³ Did that which is good, then, become death to me? By no means! Nevertheless, in order that sin might be recognized as sin, it used what is good to bring about my death, so that through the commandment sin might become utterly sinful.

¹⁴ We know that the law is spiritual; but I am unspiritual, sold as a slave to sin. ¹⁵ I do not understand what I do. For what I want to do I do not do, but what I hate I do. ¹⁶ And if I do what I do not want to do, I agree that the law is good. ¹⁷ As it is, it is no longer I myself who do it, but it is sin living in me. ¹⁸ For I know that good itself does not dwell in me, that is, in my sinful nature. For I have the desire to do what is good, but I cannot carry it out. ¹⁹ For I do not do the good I want to do, but the evil I do not want to do—this I keep on doing. ²⁰ Now if I do what I do not want to do, it is no longer I who do it, but it is sin living in me that does it.

²¹ So I find this law at work: Although I want to do good, evil is right there with me. ²² For in my inner being I delight in God's law; ²³ but I see another law at work in me, waging war against the law of my mind and making me a prisoner of the law of sin at work within me. ²⁴ What

a wretched man I am! Who will rescue me from this body that is subject to death? ²⁵ Thanks be to God, who delivers me through Jesus Christ our Lord!

So then, I myself in my mind am a slave to God's law, but in my sinful nature a slave to the law of sin." Romans 7:12-25 NIV

Notes for the day:

DAY 10

SIN MAKES A BETTER TESTIMONY!

SINNING MUST STOP

WHILE counseling a young Christian person struggling with the yielding and surrender of her personal desires, heart and plans to God the Father, she became frustrated. She exclaimed, "Why can't I sin so my testimony will be better?! It will show what God can do." While this was not truly how she felt as it was a burst of emotion, her statement made me stop and think. How many testimonies have we heard, to our Father's glory, of lives that were at the bottom of the barrel; but then they encountered our Savior, who through His grace and mercy raised them up to become godly believers? A lot. Does this mean Christians should all go down the wide road of sin in order that we should bring glory to God the Father?

After all, if sinning is how we can encounter God, then we should sin, right? If I truly want to know the power and saving grace of Jesus, then I need to find a really detestable sin and commit it. As a believer in Christ, He will be there to help me through it, and just think of all that I will learn about God the Father in the process! Sinning, therefore, is the way to deepen my personal relationship with Him. Let's get sinning!!

Now that we have convinced ourselves of this "truth," let's examine one small passage of scripture first; then, we can go off to the sin races. Open your Bible to Romans 6. Read all 23 verses, then come back and finish this devotional. (Romans 6:1-23)

So what did you find? Our earlier argument has been decimated, right? Paul is so very clear that God does not receive the glory when we choose to sin. Choosing to sin demonstrates that we are not under His Lordship. (1 John 3:5-10) SINNING HAS TO DECREASE. We cannot "cry uncle" here. It is not optional. This is a *requirement* if you are truly born again and have yielded your life to Him. (John 14:15, 23, 15:4, 10, 14) While sinning will never be completely eradicated from our lives on this earth because of our struggle as called out by the Apostle Paul in Romans 7:15-25, we are no longer in bondage to the sin nature because we are made new. (Romans 6:15-23, 1 Corinthians 5:17) We are indwelled and empowered by the Holy Spirit to decrease sinning. (Galatians 5:16-17, Acts 1:8, 1 Corinthians 3:16, 6:19, Romans 8:11, 2 Timothy 1:14) We must realize those testimonies mentioned earlier are laments of sin, not permission to sin. No one who states such a testimony would tell you to do what they did. Rather, they would tell you to run the other way from those kinds of wrongdoing!

Take Action

I echo Paul's question: Shall we continue sinning, even the "small" ones, in order that we could experience God our Father's wonderful grace more than ever? NO WAY! Pray today asking Jesus to convict you of the sin in your daily life and that He would glorify Himself more through your obedience rather than your disobedience.

Scripture

"[1]What shall we say, then? Shall we go on sinning so that grace may increase? [2] By no means! We are those who have died to sin; how can we live in it any longer? …. [12] Therefore do not let sin reign in your mortal body so that you obey its evil desires. [13] Do not offer any part of yourself to sin as an instrument of wickedness, but rather offer yourselves to God as those who have been brought from death to life; and offer every part of yourself to him as an instrument of righteousness." Romans 6:1, 12-13 NIV

Notes for the day:

_____

_____

_____

_____

_____

_____

_____

_____

_____

_____

_____

_____

_____

_____

_____

_____

DAY 11

IS THERE A DIFFERENCE?

A NEED FOR WEEPING, SACRIFICE, AND REPENTANCE

MOVIES that are referred to as "chick flicks" are often intended to draw out our emotions, specifically to make us cry. It was a good movie if "there wasn't a dry eye in the house." Admittedly a good cry is emotionally freeing, regardless of your gender. Yet there is another level of crying called weeping. Have you experienced this? When something or someone is so significant or dear to you, that its loss causes you so much grief as to make you physically fold over and cry so deeply that it hurts?

As a parent, hearing one of my kids say something to another that is hurtful, and seeing the reaction of the recipient, I consistently require the offender to say "I'm sorry" and ask for forgiveness. My intent is to make things right and help the offender realize the harm inflicted. But with our spouses, this is different. Repentance, not forgiveness, becomes the next level. If I offend my wife, she expects to hear me say, "I will not do that again." And, I do not want to do that thing again because it hurts the woman I love. Since I love her, my desire is to bless her, not harm her and I want to do what she has asked of me.

If my doctor asked me to give up soda, I would be unhappy about it, but not feel like it was a big loss. I like Dr. Pepper, Mountain Dew, Coke, etc., but I am only an occasional soda drinker. Giving it up would not be a crisis for me, yet it would require a change in my lifestyle with overt actions. On the other hand, when I was considering moving out of state to change jobs, my wife and I had to pray through sacrificing our routine involvement with our parents. By moving, we would be almost one-thousand miles away. We both had lived relatively close to our parents our entire adult lives. Removing them from our lives and the lives of our growing children seemed formidable and weighed heavy on our hearts.

Words matter. Their meanings matter. When we use them or act them out, we must make a conscious choice to select the right ones. When we make the wrong choice, bad things happen. The way in which we think of and approach our Savior is no different. Think again of my earlier "word" examples of crying vs. weeping, giving up vs. sacrifice, and forgiveness vs. repentance. Currently, Christian culture prefers and practices the lighter end of each of these comparisons. Yet the Savior seems to prefer and even require the other end of the scale for holy living. (Judges 20:26; Ezra 10:1-2; Psalms 6:8, 126:6; Matthew 7:38ff; Luke 18:18ff; Luke 14:26-27; Mark 12:30; 2 Chronicles 7:14; Mark 1:15; Acts 3:19; Revelation 2:5; and others.)

Take Action

Our sin should cause us to weep before the Lord because we have grieved Him. We ought not to just give up the easy things, but sacrifice everything we might want, have and desire to God. After all, He did that for us. As the people of God we must continually repent of our sin, not just casually or ritualistically ask for forgiveness. We must seek to abandon sin, not just make ourselves feel better about it. Pray today that God would show you and lead you to shift your thoughts and actions to the other end of the scale. Read Luke 18:18-29. Evaluate which side of the scale you are on and ask God to show you how to change it.

Scripture

"[18] A certain ruler asked him, "Good teacher, what must I do to inherit eternal life?"

[19] "Why do you call me good?" Jesus answered. "No one is good—except God alone. [20] You know the commandments: 'You shall not commit adultery, you shall not murder, you shall not steal, you shall not give false testimony, honor your father and mother.'"

[21] "All these I have kept since I was a boy," he said.

[22] When Jesus heard this, he said to him, "You still lack one thing. Sell everything you have and give to the poor, and you will have treasure in heaven. Then come, follow me."

[23] When he heard this, he became very sad, because he was very wealthy. [24] Jesus looked at him and said, "How hard it is for the rich to enter the kingdom of God! [25] Indeed, it is easier for a camel to go through the eye of a needle than for someone who is rich to enter the kingdom of God."

[26] Those who heard this asked, "Who then can be saved?"

[27] Jesus replied, "What is impossible with man is possible with God."

[28] Peter said to him, "We have left all we had to follow you!"

[29] "Truly I tell you," Jesus said to them, "no one who has left home or wife or brothers or sisters or parents or children for the sake of the kingdom of God [30] will fail to receive many times as much in this age, and in the age to come eternal life." Luke 18:18-29 NIV

Notes for the day:

DAY 12

GOD CALLS ME TO DO WHAT??

WRESTLING WITH REPENTANCE

IT is Friday afternoon. You are sitting at your desk at work. You are counting the minutes as 5 o'clock approaches. Vacation is almost here. The phone rings. It is your boss asking you to come in his office. You think to yourself, "He must want to wish me safe travels!" Okay, no not really! Actually, your heart sinks to the floor and you think, "What is he going to ask me to do?" And sure enough, after you enter the office he announces there has been a big problem, and you need to cancel your vacation.

As a growing Christian, you have probably experienced this same feeling when sitting in a Bible study or listening to a sermon. In that moment, God revealed some new discovery of what He requires of you to be obedient. Your thoughts likely raced to how you could do that, why you had to do it or even what the steps were to actually accomplish it. Maybe you have experienced this while reflecting on repentance this week.

Repentance is a robust and penetrating word and carries a very obvious and clear expectation. It is required for revival to come and put a new and fresh song in our heart. (Psalm 40:3) 2 Chronicles 7:14 NIV is a word from the Lord to King Solomon. The Lord said, "If my people, who are called by my name, will humble themselves and pray and seek my face and turn from their wicked ways (repent), then will I hear from heaven and will forgive their sin and will heal their land." The Lord Himself declares that the path to revival requires humility, prayer, yielding and repentance.

Take Action

If you have been struggling with this concept of repentance, listen to the voice of God calling you to surrender and yield more of your time, thinking and effort to comprehending His heart and mind. A revival of your heart, mind and life will bring thirty, sixty or hundred-fold of blessings upon you. (Psalms 112:1, Luke 11:28) If you are not struggling with this, but know someone who is, then pray for them.

Read the story of Jacob and his wrestling with the Lord in Genesis 32:22-32. Pray that God will meet with you, lift this burden, strengthen you to accomplish His agenda and bless you because of your repentance and fresh surrender to His will and renewed yielding to His voice.

Scripture

²² That night Jacob got up and took his two wives, his two female servants and his eleven sons and crossed the ford of the Jabbok. ²³ After he had sent them across the stream, he sent over all his possessions. ²⁴ So Jacob was left alone, and a man wrestled with him till daybreak. ²⁵ When the man saw that he could not overpower him, he touched the socket of Jacob's hip so that his hip was wrenched as he wrestled with the man. ²⁶ Then the man said, "Let me go, for it is daybreak."

But Jacob replied, "I will not let you go unless you bless me."

²⁷ The man asked him, "What is your name?"

"Jacob," he answered.

²⁸ Then the man said, "Your name will no longer be Jacob, but Israel, because you have struggled with God and with humans and have overcome."

²⁹ Jacob said, "Please tell me your name."

But he replied, "Why do you ask my name?" Then he blessed him there.

³⁰ So Jacob called the place Peniel, saying, "It is because I saw God face to face, and yet my life was spared."

³¹ The sun rose above him as he passed Peniel, and he was limping because of his hip. ³² Therefore to this day the Israelites do not eat the tendon attached to the socket of the hip, because the socket of Jacob's hip was touched near the tendon." Genesis 32:22-32 NIV

Notes for the day:

DAY 13

I SEE YOU

SEEING TEMPTATION FOR WHAT IT IS

AS a child I enjoyed playing hide-and-seek. I liked it better when blended with Cowboys vs Indians or Cops vs Robbers. The hunt was fun, but the discovery and proclamation of "I see you!" was even better. As an adult, this took on a new meaning after watching the movie *Avatar*. In the movie, two races are competing on a remote planet for superiority and possession of its resources. Neither race saw the value of the other, and war ensued. However, one member of each race connects with each other despite their differences. A statement is made toward the end of the movie between them, "I see you," meaning, they saw beyond their differences and had discovered who the other person was inside.

Satan likes to play hide-and-seek. He does not want to be found, nor does he want you to figure him out. When he came to Jesus in the desert to tempt Him, he presented three trap opportunities which appear simplistic and legitimate on the surface: to meet physical needs, to show dependence on God to protect Him, and to give Himself honor and position. These seem innocent enough, yet there was more here than meets the eye. There always is when the demonic is involved in our decisions.

Satan was tempting Jesus in these ways to cause Him to sin. He presented issues that were authentic and desirable before Jesus in His vulnerable human state of body and mind. The goal was not to make Jesus feed Himself, prove God would protect Him or give Him position, but to ruin and nullify redemptive viability. Jesus is our "merciful and high priest" (Hebrews 2:17 NIV) If He had sinned, He would have been an unqualified sacrifice in the Old Testament pattern. The offering had to be without spot or blemish (Leviticus 4:3, 1 Peter 1:19).

Satan's end game was to take Jesus out of the God game of mankind's redemption, sanctification and glorification. It is no different with us. When we are faced with a temptation, we should say to Satan and his demons, "I see you!" We must struggle against even the smallest of temptations that lead us to sin. Sinning takes you out of the game, even if only for a brief time. It is a distraction and deviation from our primary purposes – worshiping the triune God and advancing His Kingdom.

Take Action

Read Matthew 4:1-11 and pray for the Savior to reveal the evil attacks that come against you and to provide you with the wisdom, strength and faith to walk away from the temptation. Pray and live to turn every temptation from an opportunity of failure into an opportunity of spiritual success.

Scripture

"¹Then Jesus was led by the Spirit into the wilderness to be tempted by the devil. ² After fasting forty days and forty nights, he was hungry. ³ The tempter came to him and said, "If you are the Son of God, tell these stones to become bread."

⁴ Jesus answered, "It is written: 'Man shall not live on bread alone, but on every word that comes from the mouth of God.'" ⁵ Then the devil took him to the holy city and had him stand on the highest point of the temple. ⁶ "If you are the Son of God," he said, "throw yourself down. For it is written:

"'He will command his angels concerning you, and they will lift you up in their hands, so that you will not strike your foot against a stone.'"

⁷ Jesus answered him, "It is also written: 'Do not put the Lord your God to the test.'" ⁸ Again, the devil took him to a very high mountain and showed him all the kingdoms of the world and their splendor. ⁹ "All this I will give you," he said, "if you will bow down and worship me." ¹⁰ Jesus said to him, "Away from me, Satan! For it is written: 'Worship the Lord your God, and serve him only.'"

¹¹ Then the devil left him, and angels came and attended him." Matthew 4:1-11 NIV

Notes for the day:

DAY 14

Out of this World

Struggle against evil

ALIEN visitors or invasion, that's what comes to mind when we hear "Out of this World." There have been many attempts to imagine such an event, some good some not so good. A few of the most famous are *Star Trek*, *Star Wars*, and the original *War of the Worlds*. These and other movies or made for TV series have sought to convince us that we are not alone in the universe. In a spiritual sense, this is a true statement.

The Apostle Paul speaks to this in Ephesians 6:10-12. Take a moment to read these verses a few times. Ponder each word and phrase. Ask yourself questions about what you see: who is he speaking to, when is it happening, what is he describing, why is he addressing this, and how can we apply it?

Our focus is all too often on the empirical: things we can see and touch. These might include tasks at work, house chores, grocery shopping, playing with the kids, etc. We even add in "causes" like saving animals, protecting the earth, mitigating racism, or extending a compassionate hand. None of which are bad to do. Contributing to society is a duty for all Christians. The problem comes in when we treat these causes as the fix for humanity. We take these causes on to fight mankind's deficiencies.

Ironically, the true battle ground is just the opposite – it is spiritual. History proves that this fight in our own wisdom and strength will never solve human flaws, failure and foolishness. We must be about the business of fighting the forces of evil that *drive* the deficiencies of mankind. Sin is the root cause and is championed by Satan and his legions. The temptations you faced yesterday and the ones you will face today are but skirmishes in a larger battle and a timeless war. We must re-focus our efforts on this spiritual battlefield. Paul is clear that the goal is to be able to STAND against the devil's schemes. Recall yesterday's discussion of how Satan has nothing but evil ulterior motives? No matter what the temptation, his goal is to take you out of the race you are running for Christ.

Take Action

Are you giving Satan the satisfaction of accomplishing his goal? Pray! Pray! Pray! Talking with the Lord during periods of refinement in the furnace will result in your endurance and His glory. (Isaiah 48:10-11) Change your focus and see what is actually happening with each event that comes your way. Prepare for battle mentally and spiritually by praying continuously. (1 Thessalonians 5:17)

Scripture

"[10] Finally, be strong in the Lord and in his mighty power. [11] Put on the full armor of God, so that you can take your stand against the devil's schemes. [12] For our struggle is not against flesh and blood, but against the rulers, against the authorities, against the powers of this dark world and against the spiritual forces of evil in the heavenly realms." Ephesians 6:10-12 NIV

Notes for the day:

Day 15

Tools Included, Part 1

Understanding the Armor of God

SOMEWHERE along the way, manufacturers figured out that not everyone has a tool box. They made the choice to begin including an Allen Wrench, Open-End Wrench, or screwdriver with the "some assembly required" products. So that the swing set goes up, table gets put together, or bookcase is built with convenience for the customer. Suggestion: when you are done getting it all together, store the tool in a place you will remember! That tool is proprietary; you will have a hard time finding a replacement should you lose it.

Spiritually, God provides us the tools we need to live as His conqueror. One of the tool lists is in Ephesians 6:13-17. Take a moment and read this passage, even if you have studied it before. Be sure to see each tool and its purpose.

The list begins with *The Belt of Truth*. It is the only place to start a foundation. What truth? That God, who is our creator, redeemer and perfecter, is the only God and is found in three entities or persons: God the Father, Jesus the Son, and God the Holy Spirit. Each one is unique, but wholly integrated as one God (Matthew 3:16-17; John 14:6, 10-11; Acts 1, 2; and others). According to scripture, anything short of this holy, providential, sovereign, triune God is a deception and a lie. So why a belt? Because it was what held the Roman soldier's uniform together and secured his sword. It was the centerpiece. Without it everything fell apart. This is the same of our Christian faith: without this understanding of God, everything falls apart. We are warned of this, see 2 Timothy 4:4; 1 John 1:6. Study the scripture for understanding of the truth, in order that you may not live your life in a myth or illusion which leads to darkness and confusion.

The next piece of armor is the *Breastplate of Righteousness*. This critical piece of armor protects the heart. This word picture shows us that living righteously will guard and protect our heart. The Lord is passionate about this because your heart belongs to Him. As we accept His gift of salvation, we are yielding and surrendering all we are to His Lordship. This process of growing under His Lordship is called sanctification. During this growth we must learn how we are to give all our heart to Him, that is, who we are: lock, stock and barrel (Mark 12:30). He wants and yearns for our affections, worship and focus. We are then living as representatives of Christ and can authentically bear His name in ours. We are given Jesus' righteousness (Romans 5:17, 2 Corinthians 5:21). Even in our failures, He will see us as righteous. (Psalms 103:10-13, Luke 15:11-24, Ephesians 1:7, and others.) We are alive because of Jesus' righteousness (Romans 8:1-11). We must advance in holy living (1 Peter 1:16).

The last tool for today is the *Shoes of Peace*. This is the reconciliation and restoration the Father offers through Jesus Christ. This salvation brings peace to individual hearts and a world in chaos. This is the cornerstone of our faith. The right shoes on our feet provide balance and sure footing for various activities, just as Jesus and His salvation does for the true disciple. These shoes will ensure you finish the race (1 Corinthians 9:24) and crush Satan in the process (Romans 16:20).

Take Action

Prayerfully consider and contemplate these three tools today. Call each one out as you pray to "put on your armor." Look for ways in the events of today to see how these three tools will protect you, help you and change you.

Scripture

"[13] Therefore put on the full armor of God, so that when the day of evil comes, you may be able to stand your ground, and after you have done everything, to stand.

[14] Stand firm then, with the belt of truth buckled around your waist, with the breastplate of righteousness in place, [15] and with your feet fitted with the readiness that comes from the gospel of peace." Ephesians 6:13-15 NIV

Notes for the day:

_____

_____

_____

_____

_____

_____

_____

_____

_____

_____

_____

_____

_____

_____

Day 16

Tools Included, Part 2

Understanding the Armor of God

HAVING the right tool always makes all the difference. Regardless of what you are working on, a vehicle engine, sewing, cutting wood or writing a paper, you need the right tool. A set of wrenches will not help you sew, a pencil with paper and books will not fix an engine, a saw will not help you write anything on paper and a needle with thread will not make firewood. A spiritual battle requires the right tools to get the war won.

Our first tool for today is *The Shield of Faith*. Like the three previous tools, this one too is defensive. Scholars believe this shield was made of layers of firm wood, covered in hide and just before battle it was dipped in water to put out flaming arrows. This is a marvelous picture of faith. Faith will completely cover us, hide us and protect us. Faith allows us to move forward in the battle. Isaiah warned King Ahaz of Judah that without faith, he would fail (Isaiah 7:9). Jesus called out the disciples' lack of faith during the storm (Luke 8:22-25). The Apostle Paul exhorted the Galatians, "The righteous will live by faith." (Galatians 3:11 NIV) Do you trust in the triune God? Take some time to review the "Hall of Faith" in Hebrews 11. While reading, remember that the power is not in faith, but in the object of faith as demonstrated so clearly in the lives of those listed there.

Next Paul identifies the *Helmet of Salvation*. Paul knew our minds were the gateway to our hearts. We must first have the proper understanding and comprehension of God and His holiness to ensure we have the correct perspective: God is Creator, we are the creation; God is the definition of holiness, we are not holy without Christ. With the correct perspective in place, we then can and must guard our minds. In Thessalonians 5:12-22 we are given at least 16 instructions on how to live righteously. One of those elements is to "pray continually." Paul repeats this again in the Ephesians 6 passage. Prayer seeking to dialogue with Him without ceasing and in all things will defend us against temptations and rightly order our choices and responses. Temptation comes to the mind first, and then the choice to sin sullies and distracts our heart. He will direct our paths as we must never lean on our own understanding (Proverbs 3:5-6).

The last tool Paul discusses here is the *Sword of the Spirit*. This is the only offensive tool in the list. For the

Roman soldier this sword was only a few feet long and intended for hand-to-hand combat. This is why some would argue this is also a defensive tool. In either case, this is not a missile you fire from your *Lazy Boy* chair. Each of us is called by our Commander to enter our field of spiritual battle (Mt. 28: 16-20). We will encounter hand-to-hand combat with demonic forces (1 Pt. 5:8). The Word of God, the Bible, is our sword. We must hide the Word in our heart (Ps. 119:11) in order for it to be available when needed (see Jesus' scripture memory example in Matthew 4:1-11). No solider would engage in battle without his weapon. As a Christian, we must not attempt to engage in this spiritual battle without our sword. The "Battle Psalm" of King David in Psalm 18 says it is God the Father who will enable us to stand, train our hands for battle, and give us strength for the fight. Are you training with your sword?

Paul wraps up this passage and these tools with *Prayer*. Prayer is critical to the Christian warrior. In any battle, communication is the one single element that determines the outcome of the fight. Military history of victory or defeat shouts this lesson to us. Dr. H.D. McCarty said, "Uncompromised communication (our dialogue with our Lord) is urgent, crucial and determinative in spiritual warfare!" We must clearly hear the voice of the Holy Spirit to appropriately use these tools and fight the right fight.

Take Action

Spend time with the Lord discussing these tools and their application to your life. Make a commitment to routinely put on the armor of God. Tell someone of this commitment and ask them to hold you accountable by asking how it was applied in your life each week.

Scripture

"[16] In addition to all this, take up the shield of faith, with which you can extinguish all the flaming arrows of the evil one. [17] Take the helmet of salvation and the sword of the Spirit, which is the word of God. [18] And pray in the Spirit on all occasions with all kinds of prayers and requests. With this in mind, be alert and always keep on praying for all the Lord's people. Ephesians 6:16-18 NIV

Notes for the day:

_____
_____
_____
_____
_____
_____
_____
_____
_____
_____
_____
_____
_____
_____
_____
_____
_____
_____

Day 17

No One is an Island

The church is an army who can win together

When someone passes away we gather together. When someone loses their job we gather together. When any deep crisis comes we look to others for comfort, encouragement and strength. Banding together provides the knowledge that we are not alone, that we do not have to bear the burden by ourselves. When we are fighting this good fight of faith and we struggle, we must seek the Father more earnestly and band together with His people.

No war was ever won by one man alone. It takes a trained, unified and committed army to accomplish conquering. God has put together the body of believers to work together as one unit under His command. This church, the Bride of Christ, is called to worship and serve together. We are one body made up of many parts, each created and placed in the body for a specific work

(Romans 12:6-8; 1 Corinthians 12:12-31). Together is how the task is accomplished.

We are never to stop coming together (Hebrews 10:25). As a body of believers who encourage one another *daily*, we strive to not be overtaken by sin (Hebrews. 3:13). When you need a helping hand, listening ear, or prayers spoken, look to fellow believers in His church. The New Testament church found in Acts 4:32-37 was a community. They supported each other. They protected each other. They met each other's needs.

As you repent and your mind changes about the foolishness of your sins, daily put on the armor of God, and more vigorously run your race, look to your church for necessary support in this journey. Others will be looking too, and some at you. Band together as you and your church prepare for revival. Make time to pray with others during this week for the revival event. God will give forgiveness in your repentance, strengthen you to resist temptations, and encourage your heart with those around you in the church.

Take Action

Call, text or email someone and ask them to meet you for prayer today. When you meet call on the Lord for His anointing and presence! Pray for yourselves, each other, leadership, the church family and the revival.

Scripture

"³² All the believers were one in heart and mind. No one claimed that any of their possessions was their own, but they shared everything they had. ³³ With great power the apostles continued to testify to the resurrection of the Lord Jesus. And God's grace was so powerfully at work in them all ³⁴ that there were no needy persons among them. For from time to time those who owned land or houses sold them, brought the money from the sales ³⁵ and put it at the apostles' feet, and it was distributed to anyone who had need." Acts 4:32-35 NIV

Notes for the day:

_____
_____
_____
_____
_____
_____
_____
_____
_____
_____
_____
_____
_____
_____
_____
_____

Day 18

The Power of Prayer

Pray to discover and move to His will

THERE I was, at the age of 13, laying in the emergency room with a team of doctors trying desperately to save my life. I had been run over by a pickup truck while riding my bike. My heart rate was sporadic at best! I was D.O.A. on and off all the way to the hospital. In fact, after three and half hours of surgery, my heart stopped beating. The medical staff informed my parents I had passed away. Immediately my dad started calling family and church leaders.

Within about a half an hour, a prayer chain stretching across the continental United States had been strung together. The result: a heart-beat! My heart monitor had accidentally been left running after the medical team pronounced me dead, and after about 10-15 minutes, the surgeon grew tired of hearing the flat-line tone. He went in to unplug the machine, and a spark of energy, which is not supposed to be possible from the monitor, re-ignited my heart. A few hours later, I was rolled out into the recovery room and after only a few months of therapy I was physically functioning normally. It was a miracle through prayer.

Evidently, the Savior had more for me. My life is truly His. I share and preach the gospel of Jesus Christ as many times as our redeemer affords me. He has placed a burden on my heart for Christians to be revitalized, to be awakened to His splendor and holiness and to live in His empowering presence. Prayer is the vehicle through which revitalization is obtained. You do not need, nor do I recommend, a near death experience to discover your value to the Creator. The Father sent His Son to die for and because of your sin. Your response is to be repentant of your sin, relinquish of all you are and have, and rejoice in the abundant life He has for you!

Effective prayer brings us in line with God's will. We do not pray to convince God of what He should do. Prayer is a faith action of obedience for you to praise Him, lay down your burdens, intercede for others and thank Him from your heart and with your mind. Prayer keeps our focus on Him, what He is doing and how or where we can join His activity. Pray continually! This is how you protect your mind and heart. This is how you can encourage others.

Prayer is our dialogue with the Father, sharing all of life with Him. In prayer we share our thoughts, fears, joy's, weaknesses, love, difficulties, and successes. In doing so, we will be given the Messiah's mind. His purpose, peace and power will become ours. We will want what He wants. We will see the world as He sees it. We will develop an authentic desire for His cross and our hearts will become yielded to His lordship.

Some say that prayer has three answers: yes, no and not now. Whatever the answer, we know for sure that God is sovereign to accomplish His will in His own perfect way. He knows what you need and when you need it. Healing may not come, money may not arrive, people may not change or "____" (fill in the blank) may not happen. This is hard to accept sometimes, but He is training us to learn what it is to die to self so He can fill us. He does not always give us the answer we are looking for, but He is the sovereign designer and He knows what we have need of that will accomplish His purpose through us. Remain faithful and trust. Jesus tells us in Matthew 6 that He takes care of the birds and flowers and He will certainly take this kind of care for you. We are not to be anxious about anything, but to pray (Philippians 4:6).

Take Action

Read Philippians 4:6-7. Why not memorize it this week? Pray that the Holy Spirit will help you see your role in prayer and this revival preparation. Pray big, because our God is a great God. Raise up the revival event at your church and ask the Lord to do something in your life and the life of your church beyond your imagination.

Scripture

"⁶Do not be anxious about anything, but in every situation, by prayer and petition, with thanksgiving, present your requests to God. ⁷And the peace of God, which transcends all understanding, will guard your hearts and your minds in Christ Jesus." Philippians 4:6-7 NIV

Notes for the day:

Day 19

Getting Usable

Forgiveness is not optional

Have you ever said something you wished you hadn't? Ever done something you wish you hadn't? Did you let it fester? Did you feel awkward and strained in your relationship? The answers of course, are yes! All of us have said and done things we wish had never happened. All of us have felt heart sick and experienced how it made the relationship useless, at least for a time. Regardless of who was wrong in that situation, holding on to it has been, or maybe is currently, eating at you on the inside.

Before we can bring our sacrifice, worship, or service to our Savior we must make things right with others in order to be right with Him. Unforgiveness is a poison. It is a sin because it is disobedience which breaks our fellowship with God. God cannot work in you or in your church if there is unforgiveness. Satan is cheering for his victory as he has accomplished his goal of taking you and maybe even your church out of the game. Jesus, in Matthew 5:23-24, is clear about how we are to approach the Father.

We are commanded to forgive as He has forgiven us. The power of His forgiveness to us is experientially conditional upon our forgiveness of others. Meditate on Matthew 6:14-15. Need motivation to get over your issue? This passage will more than provide it. Christians all too often treat forgiveness as optional, but it is not. It is essential to becoming Christ-like. Forgiveness is freedom! When we do what Jesus did and does, we will be living the Truth of the cross and only that Truth can set us free (John 8:32). Freedom to worship our Lord, to love one another and freedom from the grasp of Satan in our lives. Forgiveness is the root to the freedom of having authority over your life.

There is also no limit on the forgiveness we are to give. Now, we are going too far, you might be thinking! Nope! Not at all. Jesus tells us "not seven times, but seventy-seven times" in Matthew 18:22 NIV. This numerical reference was a Hebrew mathematical picture of never ending. Did God allow His Son to die on a cross for the sin of humanity? Yes! His forgiveness is without concern for the depth of sacrifice. Here in Matthew 18 Jesus relates a parable of a servant, who after being forgiven a debt he could not pay, went to a lesser servant and extracted payment for a smaller debt he could not pay. The King sent for him, withdrew his forgiveness, and punished him severely. He declares "This is how my heavenly Father will treat each of you unless you forgive your brother or sister from your heart." (Matthew 18:35 NIV) Read the story. It is riveting.

Jesus also said, "Forgive us our debts, as we also have forgiven our debtors." (Matthew 6:12 NIV) The common thread is obvious. Take a look at Ephesians 4:32 NIV, "Be kind and compassionate to one another, **forgiving** each other, just as in Christ God forgave you." There it is again. It is inescapable. It must be adamantly stated that our responsibility is to always seek to forgive. What the other person does is between them and their Lord. You have been obedient to the law of love by offering the forgiveness.

A Christian is never more like Christ Jesus than when he/she forgives a person who has hurt them most.

Take Action

Do you want revival? Does your church want revival? Let us forgive one another, deeply from the heart, and watch the Father's glory pour out! Pray today that God will show you who you need to forgive, then find them and forgive them before the sun sets.

Scripture

[23] "Therefore, if you are offering your gift at the altar and there remember that your brother or sister has something against you, [24] leave your gift there in front of the altar. First go and be reconciled to them; then come and offer your gift." Matthew 5:23-24 NIV

Notes for the day:

Day 20

The Rules

Which rules are you living by?

MANY homes have a chores chart posted in their house, teachers post rules for the classroom, and companies hand out employee handbooks. Rules are everywhere in any civilized culture. Rules can be seen as oppressive, or rules can be seen as the means to freedom. We all like to know what the rules are so that we can know what is expected of us. We may rebel against some rules, but overall we choose to follow them because we know chaos would follow if society abandoned or disregarded the standards for living with one another.

The Apostle Paul understood the value of rules. He was working with converted pagans and they needed a strong direction for how to live as disciples. Through Paul's words to the Colossian Christians the Father poured out the do's and don'ts and liberations and limitations of holy living. Before going further, please pause, read and contemplate Colossians 3:1-17; examine slowly and look over the words repeatedly to allow them to take meaning for you.

Try to think of this passage as the bumper rails on a bowling lane. How did you score? Are you hitting the "pins of progress" or throwing gutter balls in life based on these standards? After all, scripture is intended for our transformation more than pleasure reading. We must evaluate where we stand with internalizing and incarnating this list. See anything you need to immediately abandon? Anything you need to urgently add? This is a tough list, but it is a required list for true disciples to comprehend and live, so that we may experience the power and joy of our Savior. "Direct me in the path of your commands, for there I find delight." (Psalm 119:35) Take a moment and read Psalm 119:32-40. Ponder its words. Evaluate if these words could be your words to your King. Then as you return to the passage of earlier in Colossians 3, did you notice how the Lord's rules lead to joy and thanksgiving? Did you see that in Psalm 119 also?

Everything we do, in word or deed, should be done to honor the name of the Lord. Christ following is no place for a rebel. Rebellion against the Father and His expectations for Christian living is sin. Sin is anything we think and do against Him or His commands. One rebellious act or thought will lead to another if it is not stopped. Disobedience without confession leads to a broken fellowship with the Father. A genuine cross transformed and cross carrying believer in the Truth cannot live life ignoring the Lord and believing the Savior does not matter in their daily life. Satan cheers when we rebel in these ways and continue on a path of our own.

(Enter *repentance*, stage "right") Turning from and abandoning the cancerous sin in your life is the way to turn your life around. The Lord's rules and commandments are not impossible to live by (Jeremiah 32:27, Isaiah 41:10, Matthew 17:20 and 19:26, Luke 1:37, 1 Corinthians 10:13, Philippians 4:13). We must work out our salvation, that is, learn and live the process of sanctification (Philippians 2:12). Jesus said that He came to provide life and for it be more abundant (John 10:9-10). This abundant life promise is not a prosperity gospel focused on getting what you want. Rather, it is a statement about abundant life that means joy is in the soul of the believer as they live obediently. The abundant life comes not through the things of this earth which will never satisfy, but through the comprehension and application of the realities of the Father's kingdom in our hearts and minds. The words of "It Is Well With My Soul" ring in my ears!

Take Action

Today pray through this list in Colossians 3. Christians living holy who separate themselves to Truth will bring a revival to themselves and others. Are you living holy?

Scripture

"¹Since, then, you have been raised with Christ, set your hearts on things above, where Christ is, seated at the right hand of God. ² Set your minds on things above, not on earthly things. ³ For you died, and your life is now hidden with Christ in God. ⁴ When Christ, who is your life, appears, then you also will appear with him in glory.

⁵ Put to death, therefore, whatever belongs to your earthly nature: sexual immorality, impurity, lust, evil desires and greed, which is idolatry. ⁶ Because of these, the wrath of God is coming. ⁷ You used to walk in these ways, in the life you once lived. ⁸ But now you must also rid yourselves of all such things as these: anger, rage, malice, slander, and filthy language from your lips. ⁹ Do not lie to each other, since you have taken off your old self with its practices ¹⁰ and have put on the new self, which is being renewed in knowledge in the image of its Creator. ¹¹ Here there is no Gentile or Jew, circumcised or uncircumcised, barbarian, Scythian, slave or free, but Christ is all, and is in all.

¹² Therefore, as God's chosen people, holy and dearly loved, clothe yourselves with compassion, kindness, humility, gentleness and patience. ¹³ Bear with each other and forgive one another if any of you has a grievance against someone. Forgive as the Lord forgave you. ¹⁴ And over all these virtues put on love, which binds them all together in perfect unity.

¹⁵ Let the peace of Christ rule in your hearts, since

as members of one body you were called to peace. And be thankful. ⁱ⁶ Let the message of Christ dwell among you richly as you teach and admonish one another with all wisdom through psalms, hymns, and songs from the Spirit, singing to God with gratitude in your hearts. ⁱ⁷ And whatever you do, whether in word or deed, do it all in the name of the Lord Jesus, giving thanks to God the Father through him." Colossians 3:1-17 NIV

Notes for the day:

Day 21

Hope

Revival has begun

"ON your mark, get set, go!" The kids yell this in the back yard as they race to see who is the fastest. Every time they line up each one has a renewed hope they will win – "this time." Over and over and over again they line up regardless if one falls down, if one has lost several in a row or if the dog beat them all. They line up to go again, no matter what.

For twenty-one days now you have come back to the line. I pray each study and prayer time presented you with a little more hope and excitement in your walk with Christ. God is good! Although you have reached the end of this study, He is not done with us and will not be done until we leave this earth. In fact, He is just getting a new work started with you and your church, on whom He wants to pour His revelation and power. These past twenty-one days have hopefully been preparing you and your church for the main event where we will be earnestly seeking, intently hearing and radically yielding to all the Lord Jesus desires to do in our lives.

God will provide revival for a people who are seeking Him. He wants His children to be close to Him. He wants to show His love to His family. He desires to have more of each of us. He has shown and will open new ways to new levels of Christian living. He is always ready. Are we?

Our only hope is in Him. "And hope does not put us to shame, because God's love has been poured out into our hearts through the Holy Spirit, who has been given to us." (Romans 5:5 NIV)

Today focus on the hope you have because of Jesus Christ, then pray for someone by name that needs this hope. Ask the Father to give you an opportunity to invite them to our services and for the Holy Spirit to work a miracle in their heart.

Take Action

Let me encourage you to scan through the previous twenty days of study to recall and reinforce the hope you have because of what you have learned and how you have grown. Your preparation and mine will lead us to a deeper experience with our Savior and life changing worship as we join together for revival. With a spirit of hope I ask you to earnestly pray with me for your Pastor, church leadership and yourself for a refreshing and empowering renewal in which we will experience the Lord's presence and see His splendor!

Scripture

"^{25} But if we hope for what we do not yet have, we wait for it patiently." Romans 8:25 NIV

"^{11} Never be lacking in zeal, but keep your spiritual fervor, serving the Lord. ^{12} Be joyful in hope, patient in affliction, faithful in prayer." Romans 12:11-12 NIV

"^{11} We want each of you to show this same diligence to the very end, so that what you hope for may be fully realized." Hebrews 6:11

Notes for the day:

_____
_____
_____
_____
_____
_____
_____
_____
_____
_____
_____
_____
_____
_____
_____
_____

A Final Word

IN the Introduction for this devotional I challenged you to enter these days of preparation with a pliable heart, open mind and commitment to yield and follow the Lord's leading. I exhorted you to study the scriptures presented and seek to hear the voice of the Holy Spirit. I sought to clarify that the way to bring revival in our lives was by being centered and consumed in The Living Word, that is our Lord Jesus, and to be serious students of the written word, that is the Bible. It is my prayer that revival has indeed been ignited within your heart, mind and will as we conclude these past 21 days.

None of us should doubt that our Father God desires to rain down on His creation love, hope, anointing and blessing. These are the elements we see demonstrated in creation, the cross and eternal life in heaven. In creation the Father showed His love and splendor by making mankind in His image and designing a garden to become man's home, a place where all the Godhead's purposes would be fulfilled and where all of Adam and Eve's needs would be met. Then there was sin! The couples' decision broke the personal relationship with our Creator, but the work of the cross brings hope of reconciliation and restoration for that relationship to a fallen creature. It is so simple, yet so profound that many Christians, in their feeble cross carrying, miss its fullness. We receive the blessings which pour out from our Messiah even though we do not deserve them. This blessed life provides us faith, strength and perseverance. And at the end of our time or the end of time itself, whichever comes first, we will be fully endowed with heavenly blessing as we worship our Lord Jesus Christ singing, "Worthy is the Lamb, who was slain, to receive power and wealth and wisdom and strength and honor and glory and praise!" (Revelation 5:12)

Pray with me for this Truth to be realized in life application by all Christians who read this revival preparation guide, in order that by living holy revival may begin in their hearts, overcome their church and pour into the communities of our nation. Together, with your body of believers, we must pray for God the Father to come down upon our meeting in all His glory, splendor and holiness! We will then be able to sing *How Great Thou Art* with a full heart and sincere mind as our lives reflect our Savior and other souls are redeemed and restored. Pray without ceasing for a Spiritual Awakening.

www.ingramcontent.com/pod-product-compliance
Lightning Source LLC
Chambersburg PA
CBHW071406290426
44108CB00014B/1708